Funny Faces

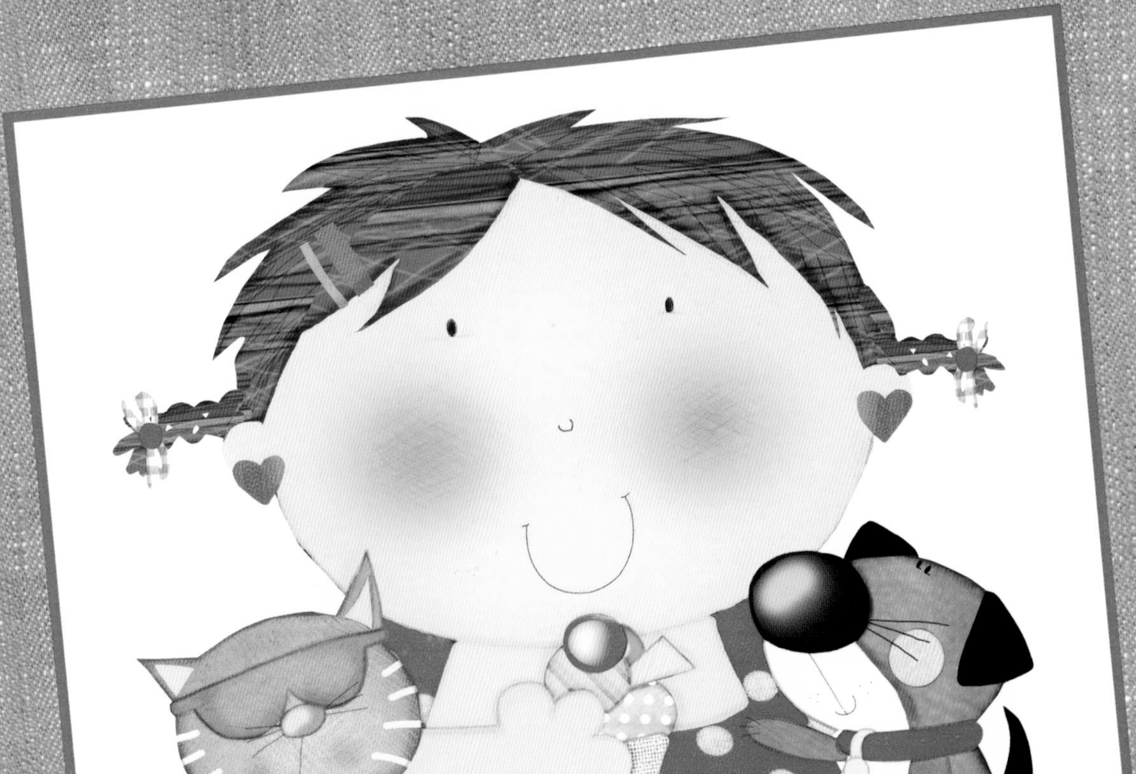

Parragon

Bath New York Singapore Hong Kong Cologne Delhi Melbourne

When I'm sad
I cry.

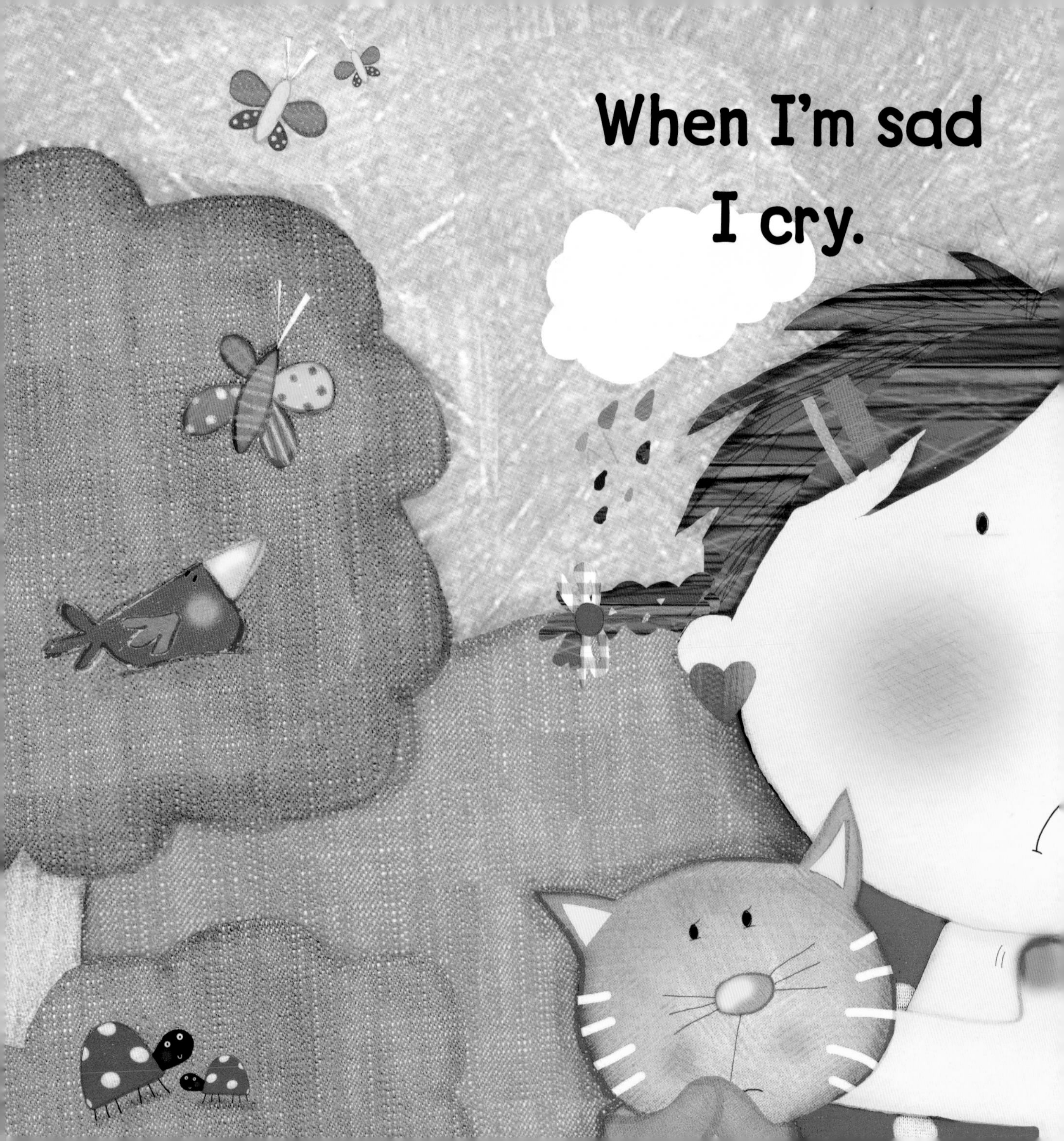

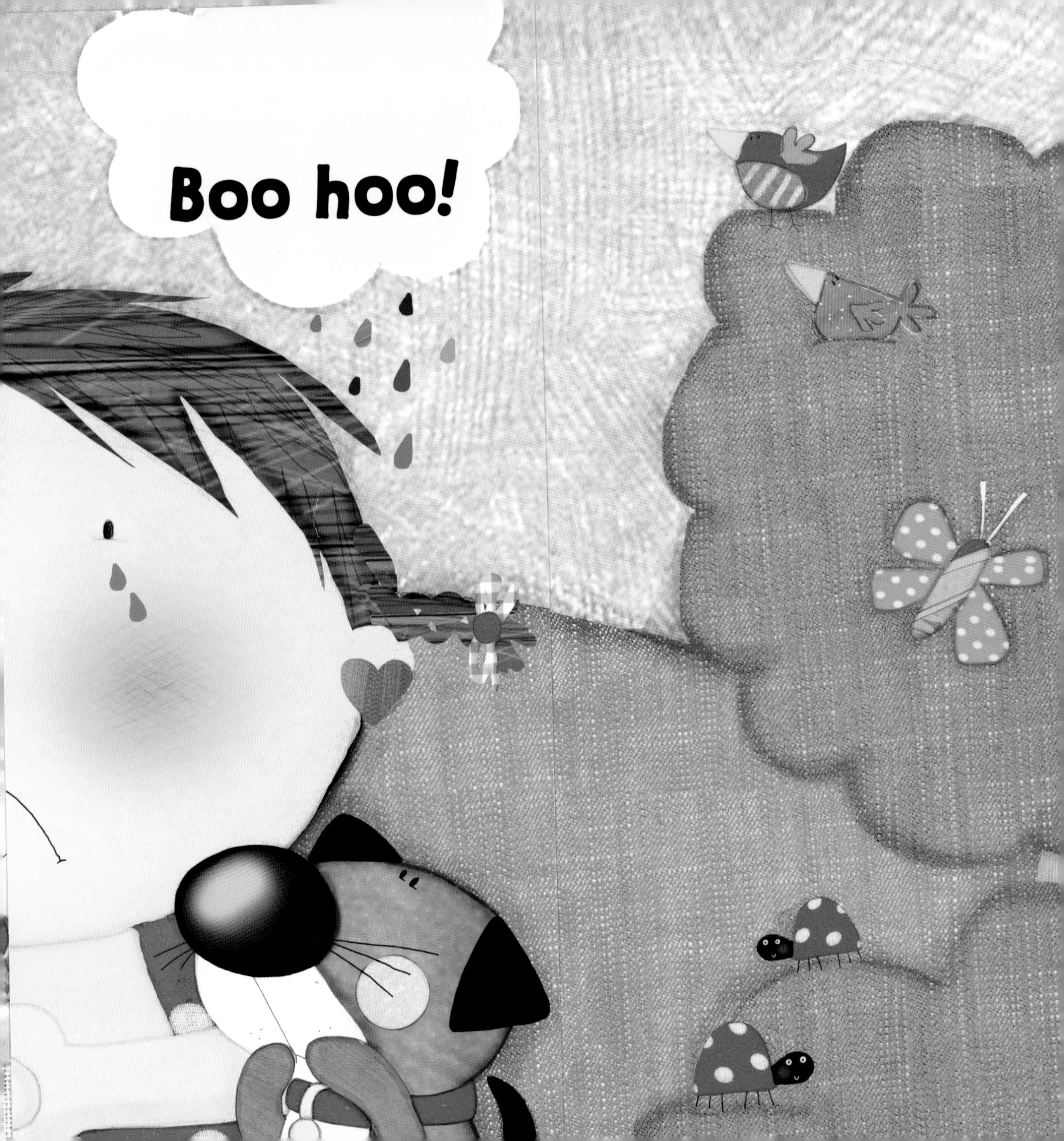
Boo hoo!

Here's my silly face.

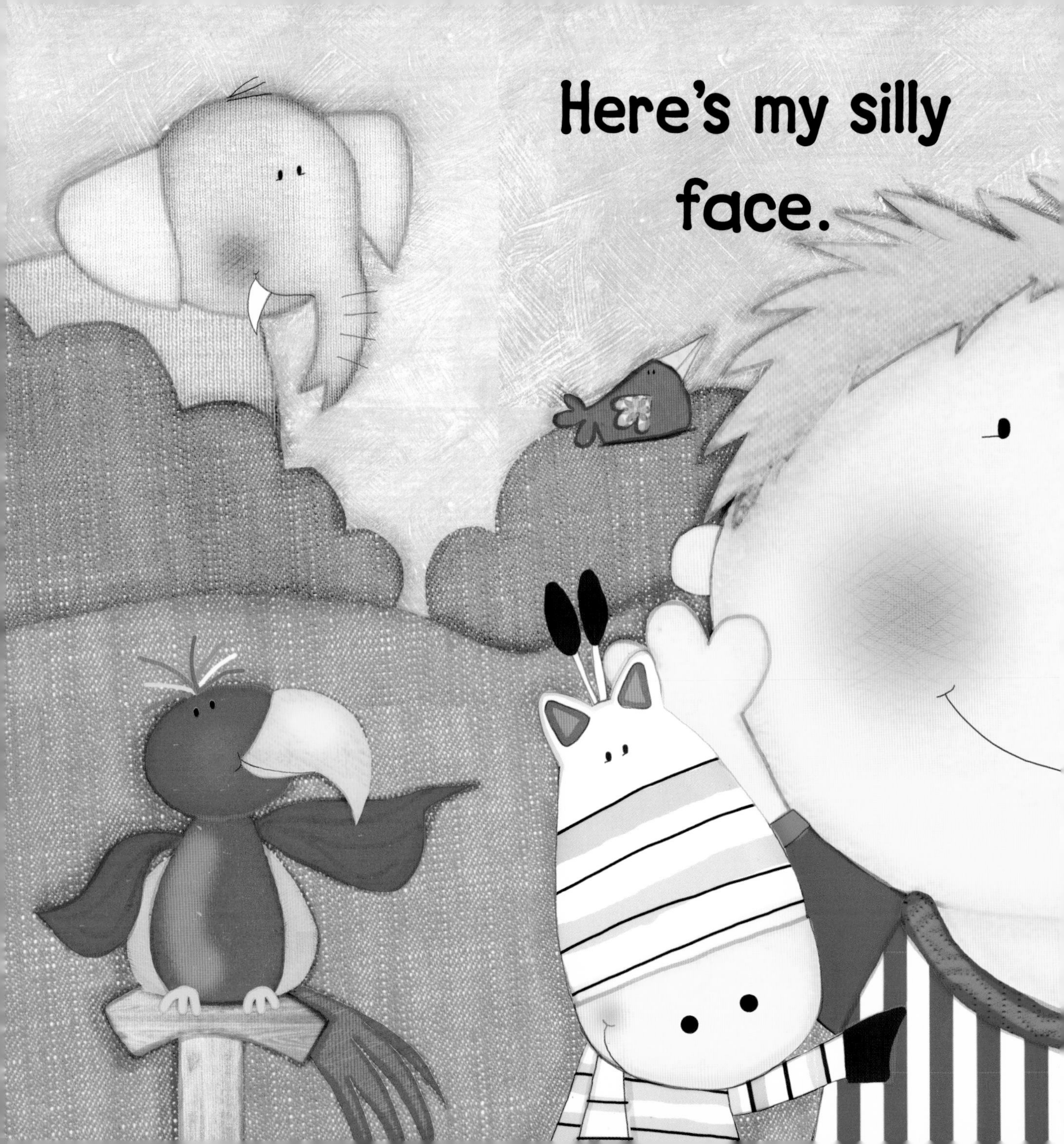

Hee, hee!

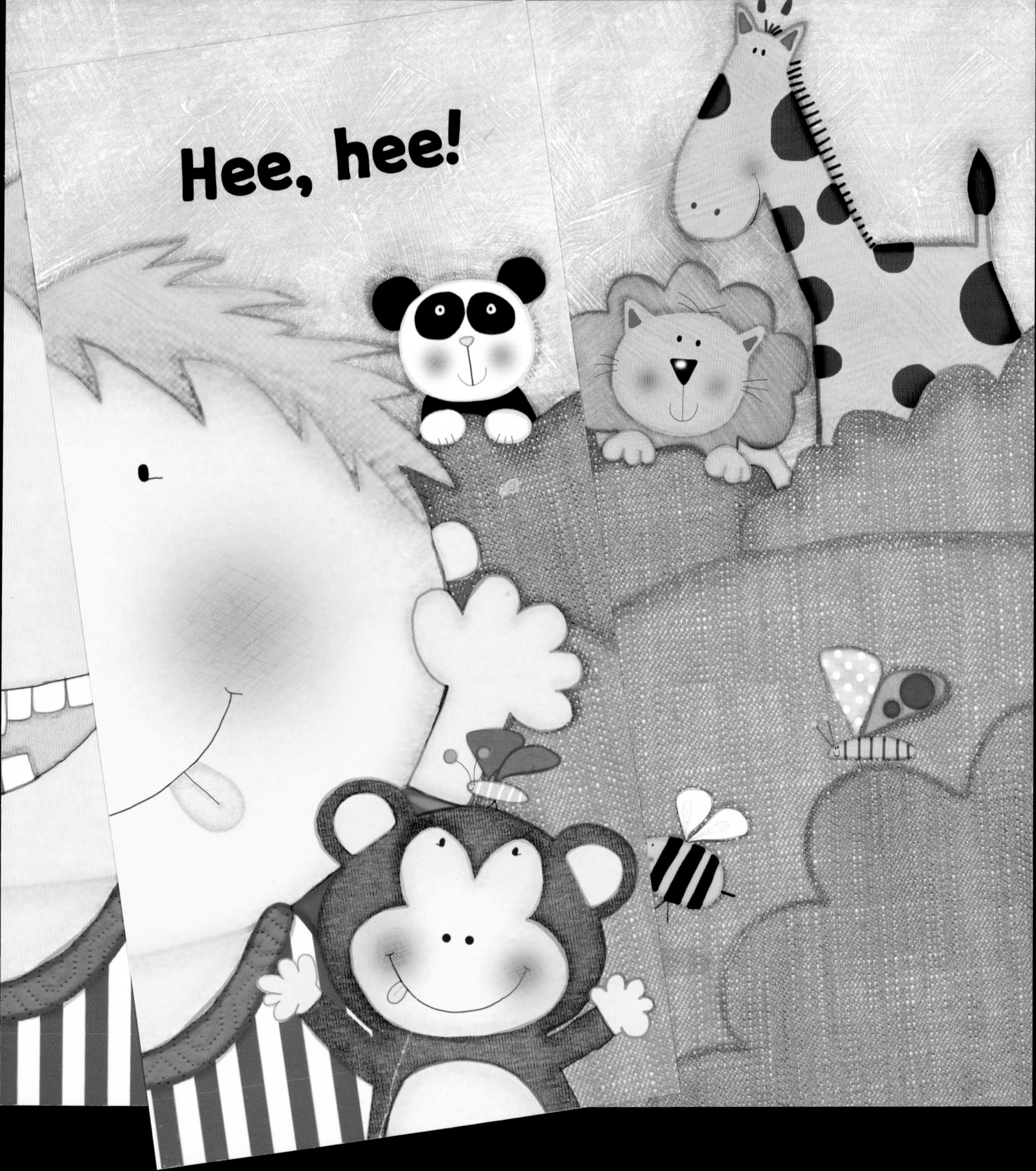

I can hide my face. . .

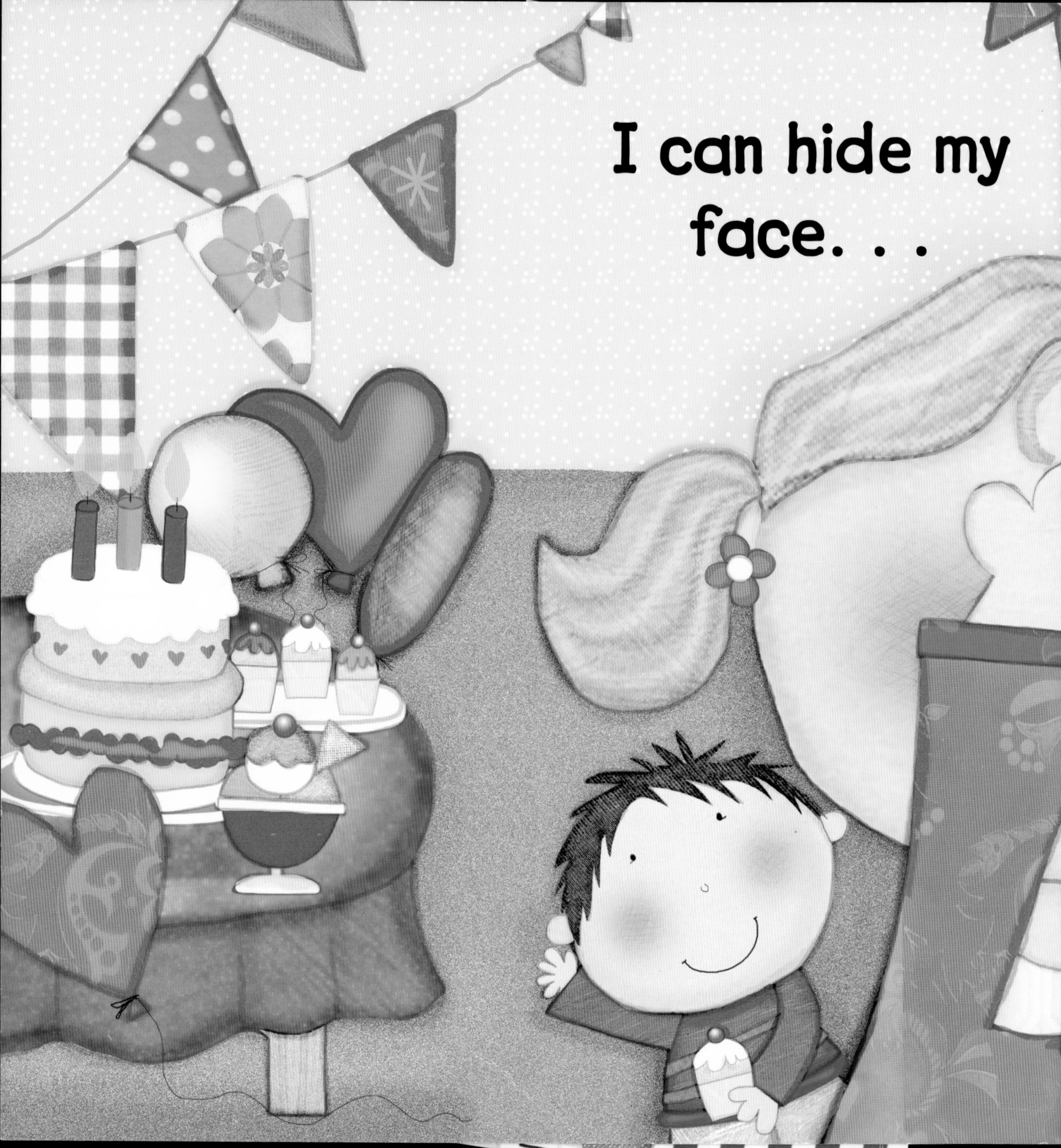

Like this!

o!

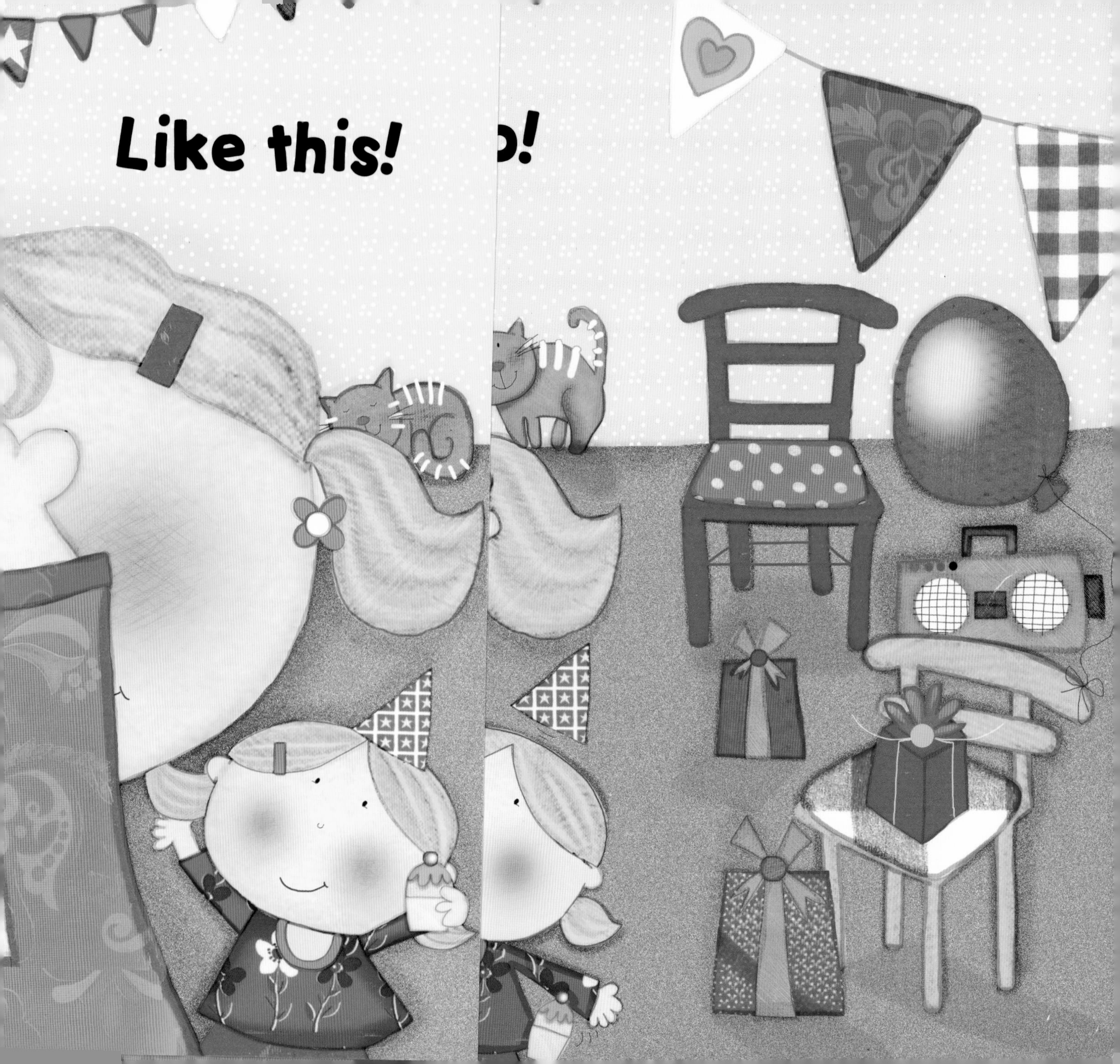

I can sing.

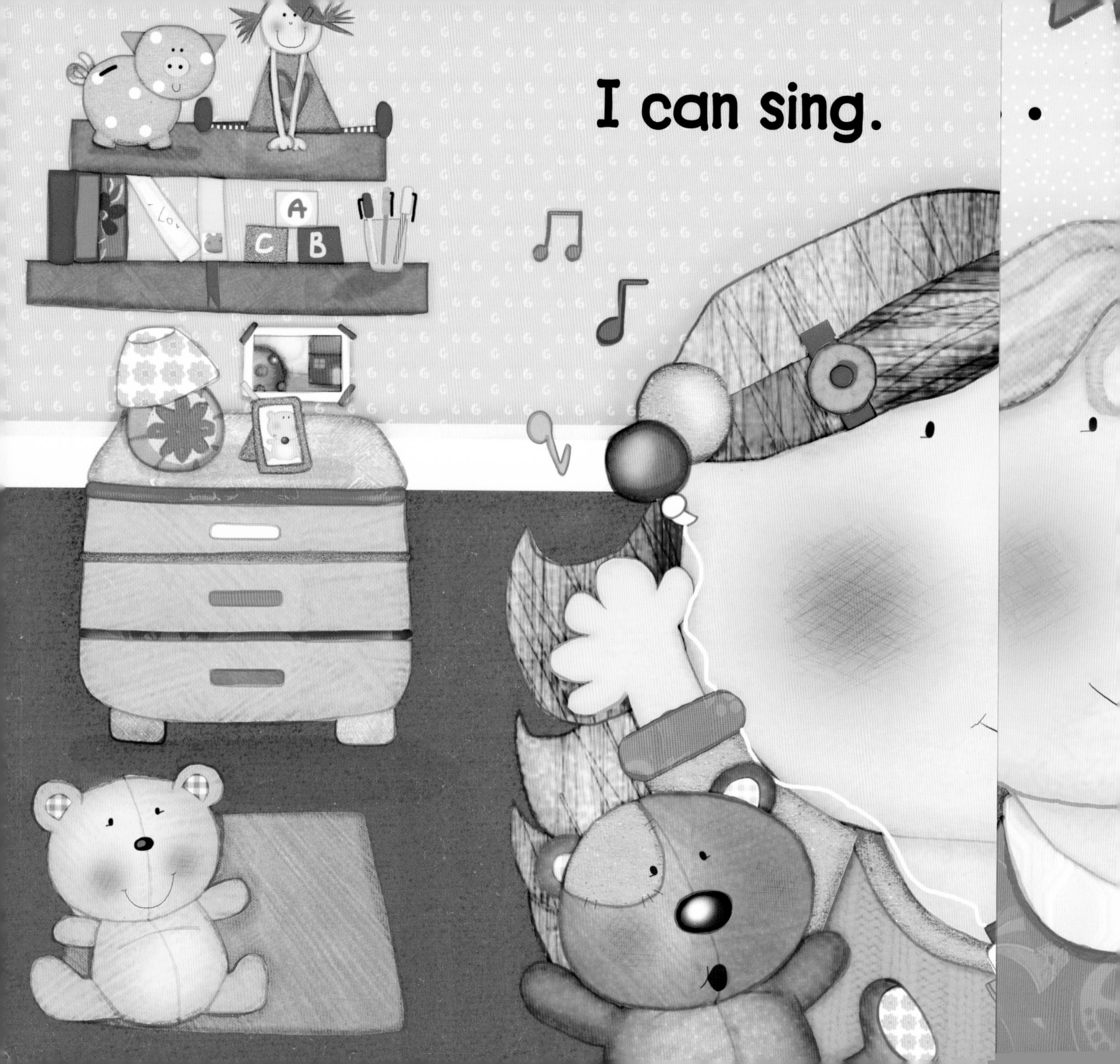

La, la!

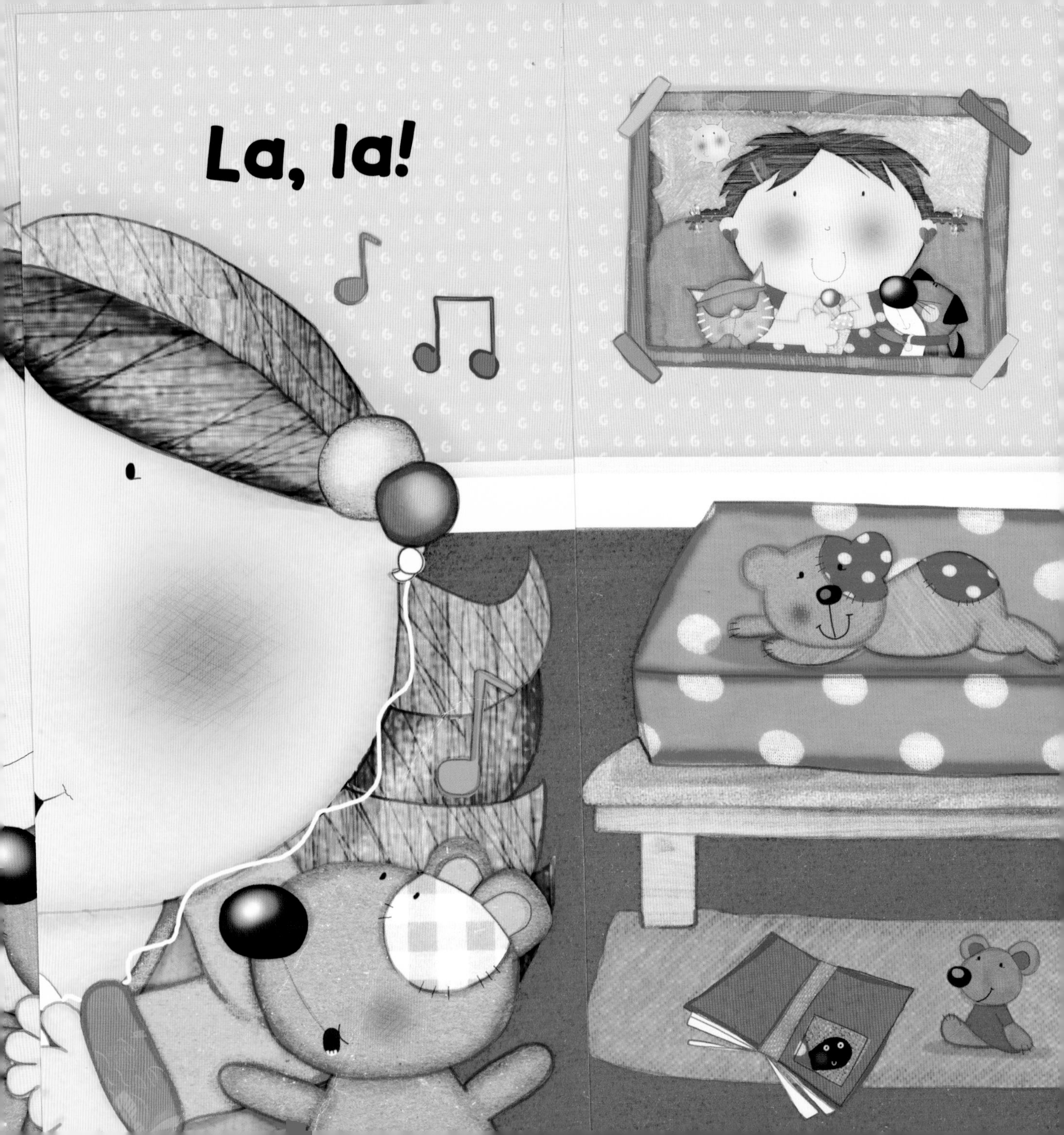

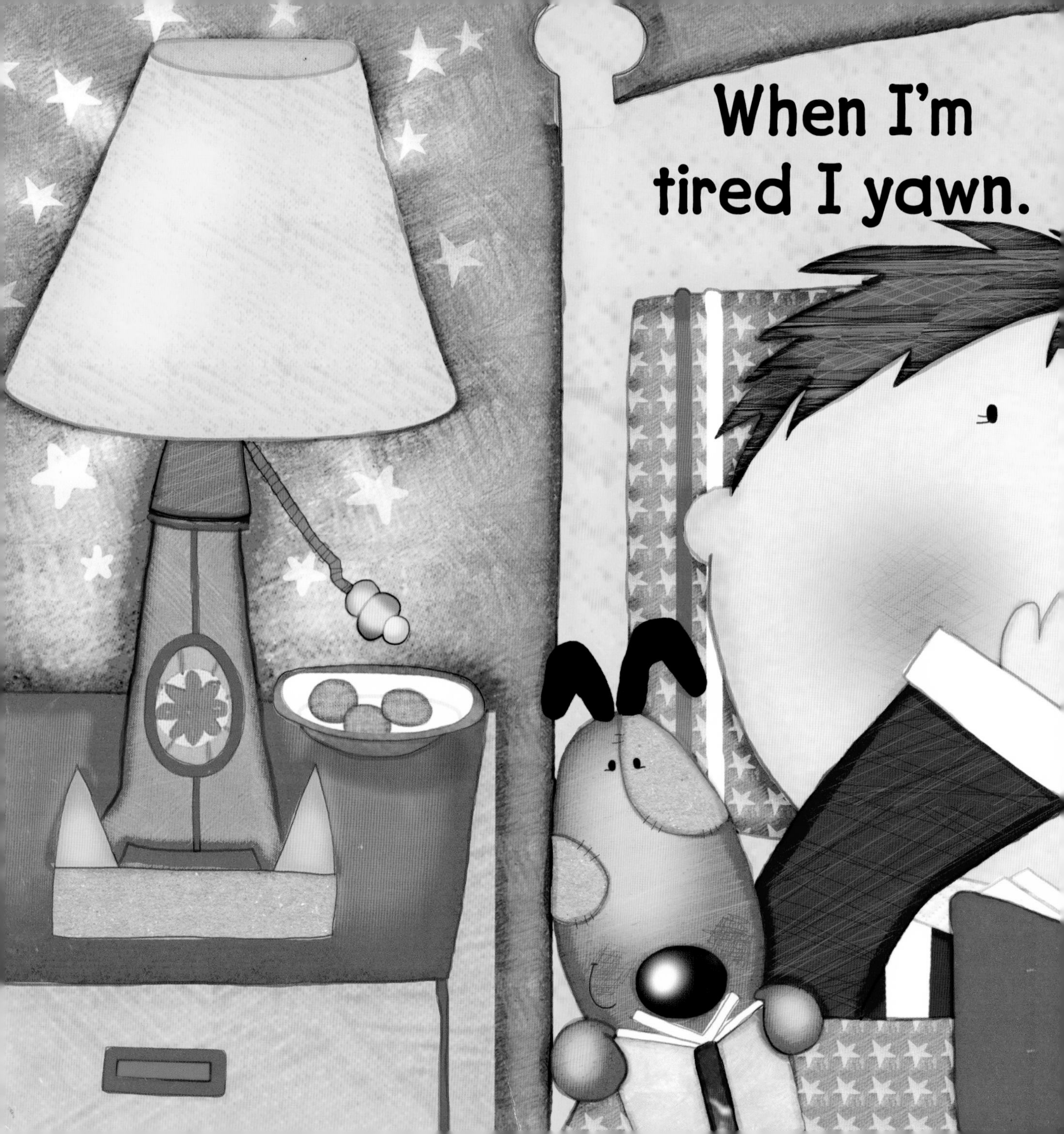
When I'm
tired I yawn.